QUIZ TIME

HISTORY & CULTURE

V&S PUBLISHERS

Published by:

V&S PUBLISHERS

F-2/16, Ansari road, Daryaganj, New Delhi-110002
☎ 23240026, 23240027 • *Fax:* 011-23240028
Email: info@vspublishers.com • *Website:* www.vspublishers.com

Regional Office : Hyderabad
5-1-707/1, Brij Bhawan (Beside Central Bank of India Lane)
Bank Street, Koti, Hyderabad - 500 095
☎ 040-24737290
E-mail: vspublishershyd@gmail.com

Branch Office : Mumbai
Jaywant Industrial Estate, 1st Floor–108, Tardeo Road
Opposite Sobo Central Mall, Mumbai – 400 034
☎ 022-23510736
E-mail: vspublishersmum@gmail.com

Follow us on: **t** **f** **in**

DISCLAIMER

Printed at Repro Knowledgecast Limited, Thane

Publisher's Note

In accordance with its name, **V&S Publishers** is known for books of **Value** and **Substance** pertaining to every possible subject of general interest, such as: Personality Development, Health and Nutrition, Management Studies, Children Encyclopaedia, Storybooks, Science books for school students, Dictionaries on Physics, Chemistry Biology, Economics, Mathematics, etc. **Quiz Time** is a decade-old series containing best-sellers in Quizzing titles. This book, *Quiz Time-History & Culture* is another addition to this series.

The book includes an exclusive collection of more than **500 informative, interesting and brain teasing questions** along with their **answers** on:

- ❖ Literature
- ❖ History
- ❖ Geography
- ❖ Sports
- ❖ Cinema

The book aims to educate and enlighten all its readers, particularly the student section and the ones studying hard to crack various competitive examinations.

Contents

LITERATURE

Q-1. Who wrote the original 'Panchatantra'?

Ans. Vishnu Sharma

Q-2. Who wrote the famous novel 'Devdas', which is made into movies in many Indian Languages?

Ans. Sharat Chandra Chattopadhyay

Sarat Chandra Chattopadhyay

Q-3. Satyajit Ray directed the film 'Sonar Kella'. Who wrote the book?

Ans. Satyajit Ray

Q-4. Rabindranath Tagore won the Nobel Prize for writing which book?

Ans. Gitanjali

Q-5. Who wrote 'Meghadutam'?

Ans. Kalidas

Q-6. Which Indian Prime Minister is also a poet?

Ans. Atal Bihari Vajpayee

Q-7. Ruskin Bond's creation – Rusty, often visited this place. Which place is it?

Ans. Dehra

Q-8. Which Indian writer has a National Park named after him?

Ans. Jim Corbett

Jim Corbett

Q-9. R.K.Narayan has his stories placed around which imaginary place?

Ans. Malgudi

Q-10. Which are the epics that are of great historical importance and tell us about the ancient culture of warfare and politics?

Ans. Ramayana and Mahabharata

Q-11. Which is generally considered as the oldest literary work in the history of the world?

Ans. Rig Veda

Q-12. Which sage was credited for organizing voluminous vedic literature into four distinct vedas?

Ans. Sage Vyasa

Q-13. Whose greatest work in literature is 'Prajana Paramita Sutra Sastra'?

Ans. Nagarjuna

Q-14. Kalidasa had written three famous plays, viz., 'Abhigyana Shakuntalam' and 'Vikramurvashi'. Name the third play.

Ans. Malvikagnimitra

Q-15. Who has written 'Big Egos, Small Men'?

Ans. Ram Jethmalani

Q-16. What is the name of Mahatma Gandhi's autobiography?

Ans. My Experiments with Truth

Q-17. Which is the highest literary award in India?

Ans. Jnanpitha Award

Jnanpitha Award

Q-18. Who has written political novel 'Mangayya Adristham?

Ans. P. V. Narasimha Rao

Q-19. Who wrote the 'Mudrarakshasa'?

Ans. Vishakhadatta

Q-20. Who wrote the Mahabharata?

Ans. Lord Ganesha

Q-21. Who is the author of 'Midnight's Children'?

Ans. Salman Rushdie

Q-22. What is common between Five Point Someone, One Night at the Call Centre, Three Mistakes of My Life, Two States and Revolution 2020?

Ans. They are authored by Chetan Bhagat

Q-23. Who penned 'Madhushala'?

Ans. Dr. Harivansh Rai Bachchan

Dr. Harivansh Rai Bachchan

Q-24. For which novel set in the days of the partition of India did Bhisham Sahni win the 1975 Sahitya Akademi award in Hindi?

Ans. Tamas

Q-25. Which famous Indian writer wrote the novel 'The Guide', later made into a movie starring Dev Anand?

Ans. R. K. Narayan

Q-26. Who wrote 'Shatranj Ke Khiladi', which was later adapted by Satyajit Ray as a film?

Ans. Premchand

Q-27. Premchand being his pen name, what was the author's real name?

Ans. Dhanpat Rai

Q-28. What is the name of eight volume collection of Premchand's short stories?

Ans. Mansarovar

Premchand

Q-29. In which year did Dr. Harivansh Rai Bachchan receive the Sahitya Akademi award for his poem 'Do Chattanen'?

Ans. In 1968

Q-30. Which Anglo-Indian writer won Sahitya Academy Award for English writing in 1992, for his short story collection 'Our Trees Still Grow in Dehra'?

Ans. Ruskin Bond

Q-31. In which year was Ruskin Bond conferred with Padma Shree?

Ans. 1999

Q-32. Who authored 'Train to Pakistan'?

Ans. Khushwant Singh

Q-33. During which years was Khushwant Singh a member of Rajya Sabha?

Ans. 1980-1986

Q-34. Which eminent Punjabi poet penned 'Aj Aakhaan Waris Shah Nu'?

Ans. Amrita Pritam

Amrita Pritam

Q-35. For which literary piece Amrita Pritam was honoured with Jnanpith Award in the year 1982?

Ans. Kaagaz Te Canvas

Q-36. Who is the author of the celebrated children's story 'The Jungle Book'?

Ans. Rudyard Kipling

Q-37. Who has authored 'The Last Moghul - The Fall of a Dynasty, Delhi 1857'?

Ans. William Dalrymple

Q-38. Who is the writer of 'The City of Joy', based on the slums of Kolkata?

Ans. French writer Dominique Lapierre

Q-39. Who has written 'The Monk Who Sold His Ferrari'?

Ans. Robin Sharma

Q-40. Which Indian writer has won Commonwealth Writers Prize, 1994 for 'A Suitable Boy'?

Ans. Vikram Seth

Q-41. For which book did Arundhati Roy win Booker Prize in 1997?

Ans. The God of Small Things

Q-42. What is common between The Shadow Lines, The Glass Palace and Sea of Poppies?

Ans. The books are written by Amitav Ghosh

Amitav Ghosh

Q-43. Who has written 'The White Tiger' and 'Last Man in the Tower'?

Ans. Aravind Adiga

Q-44. Which work of Aravind Adiga won him the 2008 Booker Prize?

Ans. The White Tiger

Q-45. For which novel Salman Rushdie was criticised and various fatwas were issued against him?

Ans. The Satanic Verses

Q-46. Name the author who has won the British Guardian Prize for 'The Village by the Sea'.

Ans. Anita Desai

Q-47. Anita Desai's which book was adapted into a film by Ivory Merchant Productions, starring Shashi Kapoor and Shabana Azmi, in 1993?

Ans. In Custody

Q-48. Who is the author of 'Shantaram'?

Ans. Gregory David Roberts

Q-49. Which author's debut work, Interpreter of Maladies, won her the Pulitzer in 2000?

Ans. Jhumpa Lahiri

Jhumpa Lahiri

Q-50. Jhumpa Lahiri's which novel was adapted into a film by Mira Nair?

Ans. The Namesake

TRIVIA

Jhumpa Lahiri is a member of the President's Committee on the Arts and Humanities, appointed by U.S. President Barack Obama.

Q-51. This famous politician and master diplomat of Chandragupta Vikramaditya wrote a book called the Arthashastra. Name him.

Ans. Chanakya (He was also known as Kautilya)

Q-52. Who wrote 'Anandmath'?

Ans. Bankim Chandra Chattopadhyay

Q-53. Who penned the lines "Where the mind is without fear and the head is held high..."?

Ans. Rabindranath Tagore

Rabindranath Tagore

Q-54. Subhadra Kumari Chauhan's "Bundele harbolon ke muh..." is an ode to which freedom fighter?

Ans. Rani Lakshmi Bai of Jhansi

Q-55. What is common between 'Godan', 'Nirmala' and 'Gaban'?

Ans. They all are written by Premchand

Q-56. Subarnalata is penned by _____.

Ans. Ashapurna Devi

Q-57. 'Anandmath', 'Durgeshnondini' and 'Kapalkundala' were authored by which Bengali writer?

Ans. Sarat Chandra Chattopadhyay

Q-58. Who authored 'An Unknown Indian'?

Ans. Nirad C. Chaudhury

Q-59. 'Ignited Minds' is written by a President of India. Who is he?

Ans. Dr. A. P. J. Abdul Kalam

Q-60. On whose story is the film Rajinigandha, directed by Basu Chatterjee, based upon?

Ans. Manu Bhandari

Manu Bhandari

Q-61. Who is the author of 'The Bandit Queen'?

Ans. Mala Sen

Q-62. 'The Indian Struggle' is written by _____.

Ans. Subhash Chandra Bose

Q-63. Who wrote 'Two Leaves and a Bud'?

Ans. Mulkraj Anand

Mulkraj Anand

Q-64. 'Romancing with Life' is the autobiography of which Indian actor?

Ans. Dev Anand

Q-65. Who has written 'Volga Se Ganga'?

Ans. Rahul Sanskritayan

Q-66. 'Our Films, Their Films' is written by a world renowned film maker. Who is he?

Ans. Satyajjit Ray

Q-67. 'The Inheritance of Loss' is a famous work of _____.

Ans. Kiran Desai

Kiran Desai

Q-68. Who wrote the 'Discovery of India'?

Ans. Jawahar Lal Nehru

Q-69. 'Staright from the Heart' is written by _____.

Ans. Kapil Dev

Q-70. 'Sunny Days' is the biography of which Indian cricketer?

Ans. Sunil Gavaskar

Q-71. Film maker Guru Dutt's letters are compiled into a book recently. What is the book named?

Ans. 'Yours sincerely, Guru Dutt'

Q-72. Who is the most eminent poet of Hindi literature, known as the pioneer of khadi boli?

Ans. Maithili Sharan Gupt

Q-73. 'Heera' and 'Moti' are the names of two oxen in a story by Premchand. Name the story.

Ans. Do Bailon Ki Katha

Q-74. Who is known as the Nightingale of India?

Ans. Sarojini Naidu

Sarojini Naidu

Q-75. Who wrote the famous poem, 'The palanquin Bearers'?

Ans. Sarojini Naidu

Q-76. 'Ekla cholo re...' is a song written by _____.

Ans. Rabindranath Tagore

Q-77. 'Nirala' was the pen name of which Hindi poet?

Ans. Surya Kant Tripathi 'Nirala'

Q-78. Jaishankar Prasad, Suryakant Tripathi 'Nirala', Mahadevi Varma and Sumitranandan Pant are collectively known as _____.

Ans. Chhayawaadi kavi

Q-79. Who is known as the Father of Hindi Travel literature?

Ans. Rahul Sanskritayayan

Q-80. Who wrote plays like Skanda Gupta (1928), Chandragupta (1931) and Dhruvswamini (1933)?

Ans. Jaishankar Prasad

Q-81. Who has written Padmavat?

Ans. Malik Mohammad Jayasi

Q-82. Who has written Sahitya lahri, Sur Sarawali and Sur Sagar?

Ans. Surdas

Surdas

Q-83. Who is the author of Maila Aanchal?

Ans. Phaneeshwar Nath 'Renu'

Q-84. 'Teesri Kasam', a classic Hindi film by Basu Bhattacharya is based on which of the Phaneeshwar Nath Renu's stories?

Ans. Maare Gaye Gulphaam

Q-85. Who was the first woman to be awarded the Sahitya Akademi Fellowship, in 1979?

Ans. Mahadevi Varma

Q-86. A Bengali writer, she was conferred Padma Shree and Jnanpith awards in the same year, 1976. Who was she?

Ans. Ashapoorna Devi

Q-87. Who authored 'Hajar Chourashir Ma' and 'Aranyer Adhikar'?

Ans. Mahashweta Devi

Mahshweta Devi

Q-88. Who is popularly known as 'Bidrohi kobi' or rebel poet in Bengali literature?

Ans. Kazi Nazrul Islam

Kazi Nazrul Islam

Q-89. Which Punjabi writer is the author of 'Sohni Mahiwal'?

Ans. Fazal Shah

Q-90. Shiv Kumar Batalvi is an eminent regional poet. Which region did he belong to?

Ans. Punjab

Q-91. Who is the all-time best-selling fiction writer in the world, whose 78 crime novels have sold an estimated 2 billion copies?

Ans. Agatha Christie

Q-92. What is common between 'Pride and Prejudice' and 'Emma'?

Ans. Both are authored by Jane Austen

Jane Austen

Q-93. What does the initials in J.K. Rowling's name stand for?

Ans. Joanne Kathleen

Q-94. In which year did the first book in the Harry Potter series release?

Ans. June, 1997

Q-95. Which is the last book in the Harry Potter series?

Ans. Harry Potter and the Deathly Hallows

Q-96. In which country does the story 'The Pied Piper of Hamelin' take place?

Ans. Germany

Q-97. What was Roald Dahl's follow up to his book 'Charlie and the Chocolate Factory' called?

Ans. Charlie and the Great Glass Elevator

Q-98. Published in 1951, the children's book 'Prince Caspian' was the second in a series of seven books. What was the first?

Ans. The Lion, the Witch and the Wardrobe

Q-99. Who wrote the 1947 book 'The Fountainhead'?

Ans. Ayn Rand

Q-100. The Mad Hatter is a famous character of which story?

Ans. Alice in Wonderland

Q-101. Who has written 'Alice in Wonderland'?

Ans. Lewis Carroll

Alice in Wonderland cover page of 1951 Edition

Q-102. In which year was Alice in Wonderland first punlished?

Ans. In 1865

Q-103. Who gave the 'Three laws of Robotics' in the popular genre of science fiction?

Ans. Isaac Asimov

Q-104. Who wrote "Where ignorance is bliss, it is folly to be wise"?

Ans. William Shakespeare

Q-105. Which Hindi film has taken its plot from Shakespeare's 'The Comedy of Errors'?

Ans. Gulzar's Angoor

Q-106. Vishal Bhardwaj's 'Omkara' is adapted from which work by Shakespeare?

Ans. Othello

Q-107. Who is the author of 'The Little Women'?

Ans. Louisa May Alcott

Q-108. Name the book which opens with the line "All children, except one grew up".

Ans. Peter Pan

Cover of Peter Pan

Q-109. What nationality was Robert Louis Stevenson, writer of 'Treasure Island'?

Ans. Scottish

Q-110. 'Jane Eyre' was written by which Bronte sister?

Ans. Charlotte Bronte

Q-111. In the book 'The Lord of the Rings', who or what is Bilbo?

Ans. Hobbit

Q-112. Who wrote the crime novel "Ten Little Niggers"?

Ans. Agatha Christie

Q-113. If 221B Baker Street is to Sherlock Holmes, 9 Bywater Street, Chelsea is to whom?

Ans. George Smiley

Q-114. Mercutio is a character found in which Shakespeare's plays?

Ans. Romeo and Juliet

Q-115. Who wrote the novel, 'Dr Jekyll and Mr Hyde'?

Ans. Robert Louis Stevenson

Q-116. Sir Arthur Conan Doyle is famous as the creator of which popular character?

Ans. Sherlock Holmes

Sir Arthur Conan Doyle

Q-117. Which author said in 1891, "Nothing that is worth knowing can be taught"?

Ans. Oscar Wilde

Q-118. Sidney Carton is the hero of which Charles Dickens' novel?

Ans. A Tale of Two Cities

Q-119. Which playwright wrote the Crucible?

Ans. Arthur Miller

Q-120. Who wrote the 3 Musketeers?

Ans. Alexander Dumas

Alexander Dumas

Q-121. Mark Twain was the pen name of which author?

Ans. Samuel Clemens

Q-122. Which superhero was created by Bob Kane?

Ans. Batman

Q-123. Whose biography was entitled "Dragon"?

Ans. Bret Lee

Q-124. Mary Shelley is best known as the author of which literary work?

Ans. Frankenstein

Q-125. Who wrote the novel "Heart of Darkness"?

Ans. Joseph Conrad

Q-126. Which classic novel opens with the line, "Christmas won't be Christmas without presents."?

Ans. The Little Women

Q-127. Who is the main character of 'A Christmas Carol'?

Ans. Ebenezer Scrooge

Q-127. Who visit Ebenezer Scrooge on the Christmas Eve, in 'A Christmas Carol'?

Ans. Ghosts from the past, present and future

Q-128. Who authored 'A Christmas Carol'?

Ans. Charles Dickens

Charles Dickens

Q-129. Harper Lee won a Pulitzer in 1960 for which novel?

Ans. To Kill a Mocking Bird

Q-130. "To be or not to be" is the opening line of which of the William Shakespeare's plays?

Ans. Hamlet

Q-131. Who wrote 'The Rime of the ancient Mariner'?

Ans. Samuel Taylor Coleridge

Q-132. 'The Solitary Reaper' is penned by _____.

Ans. William Wordsworth

Q-133. Who, along with Samuel Taylor Coleridge, is regarded as the pioneer of Romantic age in English Literature?

Ans. William Wordsworth

William Wordsworth and Samuel Taylor Coleridge

Q-134. What was Jeffrey Archer's first successful novel?

Ans. Not a penny more, not a penny less

Q-135. Who created Miss Marple?

Ans. Agatha Christie

Q-136. Who wrote the Hitchhiker's Guide to the Galaxy?

Ans. Douglas Adam

Q-137. Who wrote 'A Passage to India'?

Ans. E. M. Foster

Q-138. Anna Karneina is written by _____.

Ans. Leo Tolstoy

Leo Tolstoy

Q-139. What was the pen-name of Charles Lutwidge Dodgson?

Ans. Lewis Carroll

Q-140. Which are the cities referred to in the title of 'A Tale of Two Cities'?

Ans. Paris and London

Q-141. Who wrote David Cooperfield?

Ans. Charles Dickens

Q-142. Hercule.Poirot is a character in the books written by _____.

Ans. Agatha Christie

Q-143. Who is the protagonist in most of the Dan Brown's fiction?

Ans. Robert Langdon

Q-144. Where does the novel, White Fang, take place?

Ans. The Yukon

Q-145. Over the years numerous authors wrote the Hardy Boys. They all wrote under a pen name. What was this name?

Ans. Franklin W. Dixon

Q-146. Which novel of Dan Brown faced bans across various countries and was criticised by the church?

Ans. The Da Vinci code

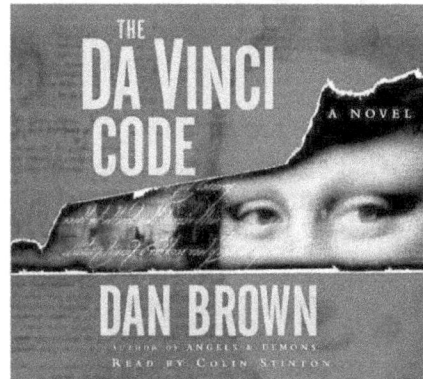

Cover of The Da Vinci code

TRIVIA

The Hardy Boys was created by Edward Stratemeyer. He also created Nancy drew, The Roven Boys and The Bobbsey Twins.

Q-147. According to a novel, what kind of animal teaches Doctor Doolittle to talk to the animals?

Ans. Polynesia – the parrot

Q-148. Which is the first novel in the Goose Bump series?

Ans. Welcome to Dead house

Q-149. Who is the author of Goose Bump Series?

Ans. R. L. Stine

Q-150. Which celebrity wrote The Last of the Really Great Whangdoodles?

Ans. Julie Andrews

Julie Andrews

Q-151. What is common between 'The hundred splendid sons' and 'The kite runner'?

Ans. Both authored by Khaled Hosseini

Khaled Hosseini

Q-152. 'Business @ the Speed of Thought' is authored by whom?

Ans. Bill Gates

Q-153. How many lines does a sonnet have?

Ans. 14

Q-154. In which century were Geoffrey Chaucer's Canterbury Tales written?

Ans. 14th Century

Q-155. Victor Hugo was a popular poet, novelist and dramatist. What was his nationality?

Ans. French

Victor Hugo

Q-156. "A man is not idle because he is absorbed in thought. There is a visible labor and there is an invisible labor." Who said this?

Ans. Victor hugo

Q-157. 'The Time machine', a science fiction work, is written by whom?

Ans. H. G. Wells

Q-158. What is the full name of P. G. Wodehouse?

Ans. Sir Pelham Grenville Wodehouse

P. G. Wodehouse

HISTORY

Q-1. Who taught the doctrine of 'Shunyata'?

Ans. Nagarjuna

Q-2. To which dynasty did Ashoka belong?

Ans. Maurya

Ashoka

Q-3. Which battle was fought between Babar and the Rajput in 1527?

Ans. The battle of Khanwa

Q-4. Who is known as the founder of Hindustani Classical Music and Qawwali?

Ans. Amir Khusro

Q-5. Amir Khusro was a disciple of whom?

Ans. Nizamuddin Auliya

Q-6. Who invented 'Zero'?

Ans. Aryabhatta

Q-7. Aryabhatta and Varahamihira belonged to which age?

Ans. Gupta Age

Q-8. Name all the four Vedas.

Ans. Rig veda, Sam veda, Yajur veda, Atharva veda

Q-9. The words 'Satyamev Jayate' in the State Emblem of India have been derived from which Upanishad?

Ans. Mundaka Upanishad

Emblem of India

Q-10. The temples of Khajuraho were built by which rulers?

Ans. Chandelas

Q-11. Ashoka called the third Buddhist Council at which place?

Ans. Pataliputra

Q-12. Where is famous Sarnath Stupa situated?

Ans. 13 km near Varanasi, Uttar Pradesh

Sarnath Stupa

Q-13. Who was the founder of Gupta Dynasty?

Ans. Chandragupta I

Q-14. In which year did Ashoka wage a battle on Kalinga?

Ans. 261 BC

Q-15. Who was the last ruler of Mauryan empire?

Ans. Brihadrata

Q-16. The Iron pillar situated at Qutub Minar in Delhi was built during the ruling period of which dynasty?

Ans. Gupta dynasty

TRIVIA

Iron Pillar, also known as Ahokan pillar, weighs more than six tons and is surprisingly, rust-proof.

Q-17. Which Chinese traveller's description about the Indian society are recorded in the book 'Fo-Kero-Ki'?

Ans. Hiuen Tsang

Q-18. Who founded the four 'matthas' in the four corners of India?

Ans. Shankaracharya

Q-19. What are the earliest examples of rock cut architecture of ancient India?

Ans. Barbara Caves

Q-20. Which dynasty is credited for establishing peace in the country after the decline of Maurya Empire?

Ans. Satvahanas

Q-21. What is the main feature of Dravida style temple architecture?

Ans. Vimana and Shikhara

Q-22. Hymns composed by which ruler are included in Guru Granth Sahib of Sikhs?

Ans. Jaidev

Q-23. Who constructed the Somnath temple after the attack of Mohammad Ghazanavi?

Ans. Bhimdev

Somnath Temple

Q-24. The word 'coromandal' coast has been derived from which kingdom?

Ans. Cholas

Q-25. What was the capital of Pandya kingdom?

Ans. Madurai

Q-26. What was the capital of Cheras kingdom?

Ans. Vanchi

Q-27. What was the capital of Videha kingdom?

Ans. Mithila

Q-28. Who was the founder of Chandela dynasty?

Ans. Nannuka

Q-29. The eighth century power struggle was among which kingdoms?

Ans. Cholas, Pallavas and Pandavas

Q-30. Who was the ruler of Vijaya Nagar?

Ans. Krishnadevraya

Q-31. The Varha temple of Mamallapuram was made by whom?

Ans. Singh Vishnu

Varha temple of Mamallapuram

Q-32. The Gandhara and Mathura School of Art developed during the reign of which ruler?

Ans. Kanishka

Q-33. What was the main metal used in the Indus Valley civilization?

Ans. Copper

Q-34. Who built the famous Dilwara Temple in Mount Abu, Rajasthan?

Ans. Tejpala

Q-35. What was the official language of the Satvahana dynasty?

Ans. Prakrit

Q-36. Nav ratnas, or nine gems, decorated in which ruler's court?

Ans. Chandragupta II

Q-37. Who introduced the famous Persian festival of Navroz?

Ans. Balban

Q-38. Name a port in the Indus Valley Civilization?

Ans. Lothal

Lothal in Indus Valley Civilization

Q-39. Mohiyuddin Mohammed is the real name of which Mughal ruler?

Ans. Aurangzeb

Q-40. Kalidas, the great Indian poet, was in the court of which Hindu emperor?

Ans. Chnadragupta II

Q-41. Who was the Nawab of Bengal at the time of the Battle of Plassey?

Ans. Siraj-ud-daula

Q-42. The famous Nalanda university was built during the reign of which ruler?

Ans. Harsha Vardhan

Q-43. Which ruler was also known by the title of Kaviraj?

Ans. Samudragupta

Q-44. Which Rajput dynasty did not surrender to Akbar?

Ans. Pratihara

Q-45. Ellora temples were built by which dynasty?

Ans. Rashtrakuta

Q-46. Tansen was a great musician and one of the nine gems in the court of which ruler?

Ans. Akbar

Tansen

Q-47. The Mongols, under Genghis Khan, invaded India during the reign of which ruler?

Ans. Iltutmish

Q-48. Which ruler initiated Din-e-ilahi?

Ans. Akbar

Q-49. What was the full name of Akbar the great?

Ans. Jalal-ud-din Mohammad Akbar

Q-50. The third battle of Panipat was fought between whom?

Ans. The Mughals and the Marathas

Q-51. Which Indian ruler built embassies in foreign lands?

Ans. Tipu Sultan

Tipu Sultan

Q-52. Which literary source details the trade information between the north and the south during the early Mauryan empire?

Ans. **The** Arthashastra

Q-53. Which Gupta ruler destroyed the Saka power in the west?

Ans. Chandragupta II

Q-54. In the fourth century BC, the empire of Magadh was greatly expanded under which powerful dynasty?

Ans. Nandas

Q-55. Where is Emperor Chandragupta said to have lived for many years as a Jain ascetic?

Ans. Sravana Belgola

Sravana Belgola

Q-56. Who was the first king of Satvahanas?

Ans. Simuk

Q-57. What was the capital of Cholas?

Ans. Kaveripattnam

Q-58. Which dynasty of the Sangam Age is first mentioned by Megasthanese?

Ans. Pandya

Q-59. The rulers of which dynasty established the largest domination in Southern India?

Ans. Cholas

Q-60. To which tribe Gautama Buddha belonged to?

Ans. Sakya

TRIVIA

Nanda, Kushan, Maurya, Gupta, Pandaya, Chola, Chaluka, Vardhana and Pallava are some of the major dynasties of Ancient India.

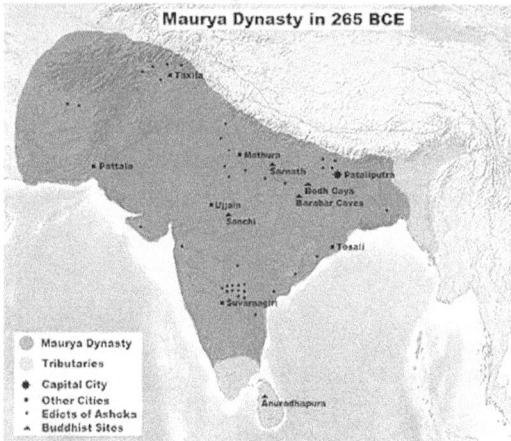

Ancient India map

Q-61. During the Governor–Generalship of whom Indian National Congress formed in 1885?

Ans. Lord Dufferin

Q-63. Who was the first Muslim president of Indian National Congress?

Ans. Badruddin Tyabji

Q-64. Where did Indian National Congress hold its first session in 1885?

Ans. Gokul Das Tejpal Sanskrit College, Bombay

Q-65. What does the Saffron colour in our National Flag stand for?

Ans. Renunciation (Sacrifice)

Q-62. Who was the First Woman president of Indian National Congress?

Ans. Annie Besant

Annie Besant

Q-66. Under the presidentship of whom the first session of Indian National Congress was held.

Ans. W.C. Banerjee

Q-67. When did the First war of Independence start?

Ans. 1857, May 10

Q-68. When was the Quit India movement started?

Ans. 1942, August 8 at Bombay

Q-69. Who was the founder of Indian National Congress?

Ans. A.O. Hume (Allan Octavian Hume)

Q-70. Who said, "Swaraj is my birth right and I must have it"?

Ans. Bal Gangadhar Tilak

Q-71. In which city did Jalianwala Bagh Massacre take place?

Ans. Amritsar, April 13, 1919

Jalianwala Bagh Massacre

Q-72. Mahatma Gandhi was referred to as the "Father of the Nation" first by whom?

Ans. Subhash Chandra Bose

Q-73. Who composed the famous patriotic song "Sare Jahan Se Achcha"?

Ans. Mohammed Iqbal

Q-74. When was the Dandi March started?

Ans. March 12, 1930

Q-75. Who commented "The Cripps Mission was a post-dated cheque drawn on a crashing bank"?

Ans. Mahatma Gandhi

Q-76. A resolution asking complete independence ("Poorna Swaraj") for India was moved at which session of Indian National Congress?

Ans. Lahore session (1929), under the presidency of Jawaharlal Nehru

Q-77. Who was the president of Indian National Congress at the time of Gandhi-Irwin pact in Mar 5, 1931?

Ans. Jawaharlal Nehru

Q-78. Who was the president of Indian National Congress at the time of Indian Independence?

Ans. Acharya Kripalani

Acharya Kripalani

Q-79. Which was the summer capital of India during the British rule?

Ans. Shimla

Q-80. "Vanar Sena", which participated in freedom struggle of India was led by whom?

Ans. Indira Gandhi

Q-81. In which year Simon Commission came to India?

Ans. 1928

Q-82. The First Round Table Conference was held in England in which year?

Ans. 1930.

TRIVIA

The Second round table conference was held in 1931, and the third in 1932.

Q-83. Who was the First Indian Woman president of Indian National Congress?

Ans. Sarojini Naidu (1925)

Q-84. The Indian National Congress split into two groups; extremists and moderates, at the Surat session. This happened in the year _____.

Ans. 1907

TRIVIA

Extremists were led by Bal Gangadhar Tilak, Bipin Chandra Pal, Lala Lajpat Rai while the moderates by G.K.Gokhale.

Q-85. In the year 1919, the British Government passed a new rule under which the Government had the authority and power to arrest people and keep them in prisons without any trial if they are suspected with the charge of terrorism. Which is that rule?

Ans. Rowlatt Act

Q-86. Who started the Hindustan Socialist Republican Association in 1928?

Ans. Chandra Shekhar Azad

Chandra Shekhar Azad

Q-87. Who is the founder of Forward Block formed in 1939?

Ans. Subhash Chandra Bose

Q-88. Subhash Chandra Bose was referred to as the "Netaji" first by whom?

Ans. Mahatma Gandhi

Q-89. Which national leader of India participated in all of the three Round Table Conferences?

Ans. B.R. Ambedkar

B.R. Ambedkar

Q-90. India's National Song "Vande Mataram" was first sung in which year?

Ans. 1896 at Calcutta (Now Kolkata)

Q-91. Gandhiji was referred to as the "Mahatma" first by whom?

Ans. Rabindranath Tagore

Q-92. Who was the leader of Bardoli Satyagrah of 1928?

Ans. Sardar Vallabh Bhai Patel

Q-93. When did Chauri Chaura massacre take place?

Ans. In 1922, Uttar Pradesh

Q-94. Who was the First foreign president of Indian National Congress?

Ans. George Yule

Q-95. Which was the most decisive war that marked the initiation of British rule in India?

Ans. Battle of Plassey

Battle of Plassey

TRIVIA

The battle of plassey occurred on June 23, 1757 at Palashi of Murshidabad, on the bank of Bhagirathi River

Q-96. Who is known as the Heroine of Quit India Movement?

Ans. Aruna Asaf Ali

Q-97. Who set up the Swaraj Party in 1922?

Ans. C.R. Das and Moti Lal Nehru

Q-98. Who presided over Congress sessions three times?

Ans. Dada Bhai Naoroji

Q-99. At which place did the British Government arrest Gandhiji for sedition for the first time?

Ans. Ahmedabad

Q-100. Who was the Prime Minister of Britain when India got Independence?

Ans. Clement Attlee (Labor Party)

Q-101. The new birth or resurrection known as the "Renaissance" considered to have begun in which country?

Ans. Italy

Q-102. What is Classical Revival?

Ans. A focus on human beings and on this life as an end in itself rather than a temporary halting place on the way to eternity.

Q-103. What were the Renaissance scholars who searched the monasteries for old Latin manuscripts that had been unappreciated and largely ignored by medieval scholars, and translated the works from Greek into Latin called?

Ans. Humanists

Q-104. From the thirteenth to the fifteenth centuries, the _____ monopolized European banking.

Ans. Italians

Q-105. Who was a great patron of Renaissance art?

Ans. Lorenzo de' Medici

Lorenzo de' Medici

Q-106. Name one of the most influential writers of the Renaissance?

Ans. Niccolò Machiavelli

Q-107. The last name of the artist Michelangelo was _____.

Ans. Buonarroti

Q-108. Which Pope commissioned the Sistine Chapel?

Ans. Julius

Q-109. Who wrote the "Divine Comedy"?

Ans. Dante

Q-110. The basic years of the Renaissance were _____.

Ans. 14th to 16th Century

Q-111. When was Alexander the Great born?

Ans. 356 B.C.

Alexander the Great

Q-112. Michelangelo was born in which year?

Ans. 1573

Q-113. Joseph Stalin was born in which year?

Ans. 1879

Q-114. When was Galileo Galilei born?

Ans. 1564

Q-115. Ernest Hemingway was born in which year?

Ans. 1899

Q-116. In Roman mythology who is the god of War?

Ans. Mars

God of War – Mars

Q-117. Who was so beautiful that "launched a thousand ships?"

Ans. Helen of Troy

Q-118. According to Greek legend, who was the first woman on earth?

Ans. Pandora

Q-119. Where is the home of the Greek gods?

Ans. Mount Olympus

Q-120. Who is the Greek goddess of wisdom, war, the arts, industry, justice and skill?

Ans. Athena

Q-121. Which order was founded as part of the Catholic revival of the sixteenth century?

Ans. Augustinians

Q-122. In which year did Columbus "discover" Jamaica?

Ans. 1497

Columbus

Q-123. A disease that killed almost half the population of Western Europe in the fourteenth century was _____ .

Ans. Bubonic plague

Q-124. Which group of people ruled Mexico and neighbouring areas in the sixteenth century?

Ans. Aztecs

Q-125. He was a famous Italian explorer of the late thirteenth and early fourteenth centuries.

Ans. Marco Polo

Q-126. Cleopatra was the queen of _____ in the first century B.C.

Ans. Egypt

Cleopatra

Q-127. The Hundred Years' War was fought between France and which other country?

Ans. England

Q-128. Johann Gutenberg is famous for inventing _____ .

Ans. Printing Press

Johann Guttenberg's press

Q-129. When were the pyramids in Egypt first built?

Ans. 2700 B.C.

Q-130. The Vikings were warriors from which place?

Ans. Scandinavia

Q-131. Mozambique was a colony of which European nation?

Ans. Portugal

Q-132. Which territory was never under European control during the 19th century?

Ans. Ethiopia

Q-133. To which country did Russia send 200,000 troops to stop its loss of land to multiple independent nations?

Ans. Austria

Q-134. Who built the Suez Canal?

Ans. Ferdinand de Lesseps

Ferdinand de Lesseps

Q-135. Which Roman Emperor converted to Christianity, legalised and supported it though never made it the official religion?

Ans. Constantine

Q-136. Of which country was Salazar dictator?

Ans. Portugal

Q-137. Which book was written by Caesar?

Ans. De Bello Gallico

Q-138. In 1945, an Allied conference decided the partition of Germany in four occupation zones. Where was that conference held?

Ans. Los Angeles

Q-139. Which sultan extended the Ottoman Empire to within 90 miles of Vienna, which he unsuccessfully besieged?

Ans. Sulieman the Magnificent

Q-140. Where did Ernesto 'Che' Guevara die?

Ans. Ecuador

Q-141. In which city did the Russian Revolution start?

Ans. Saint Petersburg

Q-142. From which Macedonian general was Cleopatra, the last queen of Egypt, descended?

Ans. Ptolemy

Q-143. What siginificant happened in France in 1789?

Ans. The fall of the Bastille prison

Q-144. During the American Civil War, who was the President of the Confederate States of America?

Ans. Jefferson Davis

Jefferson Davis

Q-145. Approximately how many people were killed in Europe by the Black Death pandemic in the 14th century?

Ans. 50 to 150 millions

Q-146. What entity did Napoleon replace the Holy Roman Empire with in 1806?

Ans. The Confederation of the Rhine

Q-147. Which English Queen was executed in May 19, 1536?

Ans. Ann Boleyn

Q-148. Which Pope launched the First Crusade?

Ans. Urban II

Q-149. Who founded the Mughal dynasty?

Ans. Babar

Q-150. From what country did Britain begin to recruit Gurkha soldiers in 1816?

Ans. Nepal

Gurkha regiment

Q-151. On which side did Japan fight in the First World War?

Ans. With the United Kingdom against Germany

Q-152. What was the original European name of Australia?

Ans. New Holland

Q-153. Which monarch launched the Spanish Armada against England?

Ans. Phillip II

Q-154. Which country lost the least men in World War I?

Ans. Japan

Q-155. Which was the first continental European state to complete its rail network, in the 1840s?

Ans. Belgium

Q-156. When did the last emperor of China ascend the throne?

Ans. 1909

Q-157. What was the capital of the North-West Territory in the modern day USA?

Ans. Chillicothe

Q-158. Which South American country fought against the combined armies of Brazil, Argentina and Uruguay from 1864 to 1870?

Ans. Paraguay

Q-159. In which month of 1945 was an atomic bomb dropped on Hiroshima?

Ans. August

Hiroshima atomic attack

GEOGRAPHY

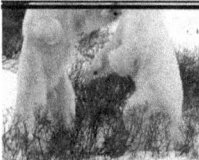

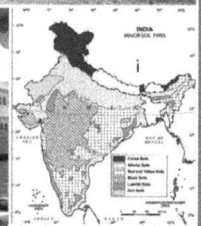

Q-1. The Nagarjuna Sagar project is constructed on which river?

Ans. River Krishna

Q-2. Uttarakhand, Uttar Pradesh, Bihar, West Bengal and Sikkim have common frontier with which country?

Ans. China

Q-3. Kavarati belongs to which Indian union Territory?

Ans. Lakshadweep

Lakshwadeep islands in a map

Q-4. Which country among Bhutan, Tajikistan, Nepal and Bangladesh does not share land boundary with India?

Ans. Tajikistan

Q-5. Name the group of islands in Arabian Sea.

Ans. Lakshadweep Islands

Q-6. Palk Straits separates India from which country?

Ans. Sri Lanka

Q-7. Which water body separates India from Sri Lanka?

Ans. Palk Straits and Gulf of Mannar

Q-8. Which neighboring country shares the longest land boundary with India?

Ans. Bangladesh (4096 Km)

TRIVIA

China shares 3488 Km of land boundary, while Pakistan shares 3323 Km of land boundary with India.

Q-9. Which is the largest state in India in terms of area?

Ans. Rajasthan

Q-10. Which is the smallest state in India in terms of area?

Ans. Goa

Q-11. Tropic of cancer passes through which state?

Ans. Tripura

Q-12. Which country amongst the India's neighbours is the smallest?

Ans. Bhutan

Q-13. How many coastal states are there in India?

Ans. Nine coastal states

TRIVIA

Nine coastal states of India are – Gujarat, Maharashtra, Goa, Karnataka, Kerala, Tamil Nadu, Andhra Pradesh, Orissa and west Bengal.

Q-14. Which is the easternmost longitude of India?

Ans. 97 degree 25' E

Q-15. Which is the southernmost latitude of India?

Ans. 6 degree 4' N

Q-16. Which Indian state is the largest producer of coffee?

Ans. Karnataka

Q-17. Which points form the West to East extension of Himalayas?

Ans. Nanga Parbat to Numcha Barwa

Q-18. Which state produces around 50% of the total silk textiles of India?

Ans. Karnataka

Q-19. Which is the most extensive soil cover of India?

Ans. Alluvial Soils

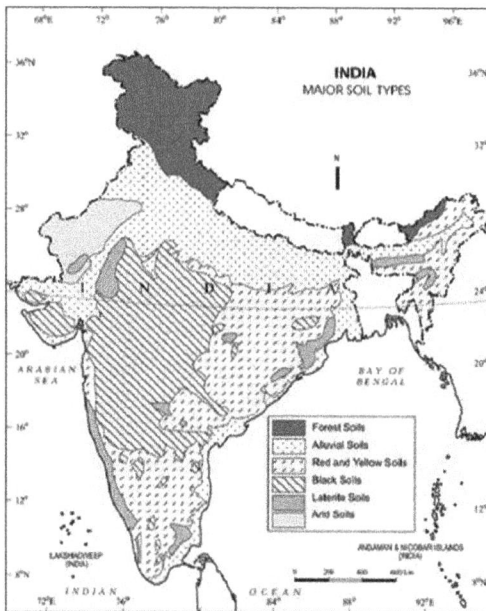

Alluvial soil distribution in India map

Q-20. The largest estuary in India is located at the mouth of which river?

Ans. River Hoogly

Q-21. Which food crop in India is sown in October - November and reaped in April?

Ans. Wheat

Q-22. Raniganj is the coal mining area of which region?

Ans. Damodar Valley

Q-23. Which Indian state is broadly as large as the European nation Greece?

Ans. Tamil Nadu

Q-24. Which river originates near Mahabaleshwar, in Maharashtra?

Ans. River Krishna

Q-25. In which Indian state is Naga Parbat peak located?

Ans. Jammu & Kashmir

Q-26. Which are the southernmost hills in India?

Ans. Cardamom Hills

Q-27. Where is the coal reserves of India largely located?

Ans. Damodar Valley

Q-28. Which Indian states leads in the production of rubber?

Ans. Kerala

Q-29. Which Indian state is also known as the 'Spice Bowl of India'?

Ans. Kerala

Kerala Spices

Q-30. Between which ranges does the Kashmir valley in the Himlayas lie?

Ans. Zanskar and Pir Panjal

Q-31. Indravati is a tributary of which river?

Ans. Godavari

Q-32. Where is Thattekad Bird Sanctuary located?

Ans. Kerala

Q-33. In which Indian state is the Pamayangtse Monastery situated?

Ans. Sikkim

Q-34. In which state is the Hydal power project Nathpa Jhakari located?

Ans. Himachal Pradesh

Q-35. The Bodo language is spoken in which state?

Ans. Assam

Q-36. In India, the western disturbances originate over which sea?

Ans. Arabian sea

Q-37. What is the length of the entire Indian coast line?

Ans. 7516.6 km

Indian Coastline in a map

Q-38. Himachal Pradesh is located in which Himalayan range?

Ans. Dhauladhar range

Q-39. Uttarakhand is located in which Himalayan range?

Ans. Kumaon range

Q-40. Arunachal Pradesh is situated in which Himalayan range?

Ans. Singalila range

Q-41. Evergreen rain forests are mainly found in regions having well distributed annual rainfall. What is the range of rainfall?

Ans. More than 200 cm

Q-43. How many islands form the Lakshadweep Island?

Ans. 36

TRIVIA

Lakshadweep means 'one lakh islands'.

Q-43. Which city is known as the 'Manchester of South India'?

Ans. Coimbatore

Q-44. Which is the longest river in India?

Ans. Ganga

Route of river Ganga in Indian map

Q-45. Sone is a tributary of which river in India?

Ans. Ganga

Q-46. Which is the largest delta in India?

Ans. Sundarban in West Bengal

TRIVIA

A delta is a marshy piece of land where rivers meet.

Q-47. In which city is 'Charminar' located?

Ans. Hyderabad

Q-48. Which city is known as the 'Pink City'?

Ans. Jaipur

Q-49. Which state in India has the world's largest deposit of thorium?

Ans. Kerala

Q-50. Which city of India stands on the River Hooghly?

Ans. Kolkata, West Bengal

Q-51. In which city of India is the famous Sun Temple located?

Ans. Konark

Sun Temple

Q-52. Which city of India stands on the banks of River Gomati?

Ans. Lucknow, Uttar Pradesh

Q-53. Which state of India has the largest area of forest land?

Ans. Madhya Pradesh

Q-54. Which is the most populated city of India?

Ans. Mumbai

Gateway of India, Mumbai

Q-55. Crude Oil is found in which place in Assam?

Ans. Digboi

Q-56. Which State in India is called the 'Land of Five Rivers'?

Ans. Punjab

> ### TRIVIA
> *The five rivers flowing through Punjab are Ravi, Beas, Sutlej, Chenab and Jhelum.*

Q-57. In which state of India is the Thar Desert primarily located?

Ans. Rajasthan

Q-58. On which river does the city of Ahmedabad stand?

Ans. Sabarmati

Q-59. Kashmir is famous for which spice?

Ans. Saffron

Q-60. On which river is the Bhakra Nangal Dam of India built?

Ans. Sutlej

Q-61. Which is the most populated state of India?

Ans. Uttar Pradesh

Q-62. In which city of India is the Gol Gumbaz mosque located?

Ans. Bijapur, Karnataka

> ### TRIVIA
> *The Gol Gumbaz mosque has the second largest dome in the world.*

Q-63. What is chiefly found at Jharia in Bihar, India?

Ans. Coal

Q-64. Which city in India is called the 'Lake City'?

Ans. Udaipur

Udaipur Lake and Palace

Q-65. What is the time difference (in hours) between GMT (Greenwich Mean Time) and IST (Indian Standard Time)?

Ans. Five and a half hours

Q-66. In which city of India is the Victoria Memorial situated?

Ans. Kolkata

Q-67. Which city in India is served by the Diamond Harbour?

Ans. Kolkata

Q-68. Where is Fort William located?

Ans. Kolkata

Fort William

Q-69. Which city in Gujarat is famous for 'Zari' production?

Ans. Surat

Q-70. Which State in India is the largest producer of Soyabean?

Ans. Madhya Pradesh

Q-71. What are the western ghats in Maharashtra known as?

Ans. Sahyadaris

Q-72. On which river bank is Goa located?

Ans. Mandovi

Q-73. Thumba in Kerala is famous for what?

Ans. It is a rocket launching station

Q-74. Name the annual fair of Rajasthan that is famous for its camel trading event.

Ans. Pushkar

Q-75. Which Indian State has most number of airports?

Ans. Gujarat

Q-76. Name the oldest mountain range of India.

Ans. Aravalis

Q-77. Which is the largest freshwater lake in India?

Ans. Wular Lake

Wular Lake

Q-78. Which state inhabits the 'Jhabua' tribals?

Ans. Madhya Pradesh

Q-79. Which Indian University is the largest residential university in Asia?

Ans. Benaras Hindu University

Q-80. What is Berar district in Maharashtra famous for?

Ans. Cotton

Q-81. Where is the Chittorgarh fort located?

Ans. Rajasthan

Q-82. Which place was once a French trading centre and is also the home of the famous Aurobindo Ashram?

Ans. Pondicherry (now Puducherry)

Q-83. Which mosque is located in the middle of the sea?

Ans. Haji Ali Dargah

Haji Ali Dargah

Q-84. Which caves dating back to 600 A.D. are located on Gharapuri Island in Mumbai's harbour?

Ans. Elephanta Caves

Q-85. Which Pacific entity is located farthest north?

Ans. Northern Mariana Islands

Q-86. With how many countries Iraq shares it borders?

Ans. Seven

Q-87. What is the capital of Bosnia?

Ans. Sarajevo

Q-88. What is the capital of Turkey?

Ans. Ankara

Q-89. What is the capital of Egypt?

Ans. Cairo

Q-90. What is the capital of Brazil?

Ans. Brasilia

Q-91. Which place in the world is famous for the Great Vishnu Temple?

Ans. Ankorvat, Cambodia

Q-92. The ancient name 'Kamboja' pertains to which modern place?

Ans. Kampuchea (Cambodia)

Q-93. The driest place on Earth is Calama, located in which desert?

Ans. Atacama desert, Chile

Atacama desert, Chile

Q-94. Which sea is not completely surrounded by land?

Ans. Arabian Sea

Q-95. Mount Everest is located on the border between which two countries?

Ans. Nepal and Bhutan

Mount Everest

Q-96. What is the largest country in South America, in terms of area?

Ans. Brazil

Q-97. Which is the southernmost Scandanavian country?

Ans. Denmark

Q-98. What is the capital city of Australia?

Ans. Canberra

Q-99. Which two countries are located on the island of Hispañola?

Ans. Dominian Republic and Haiti

Q-100. Which is the longest river or river system in the world?

Ans. Nile (Egypt)

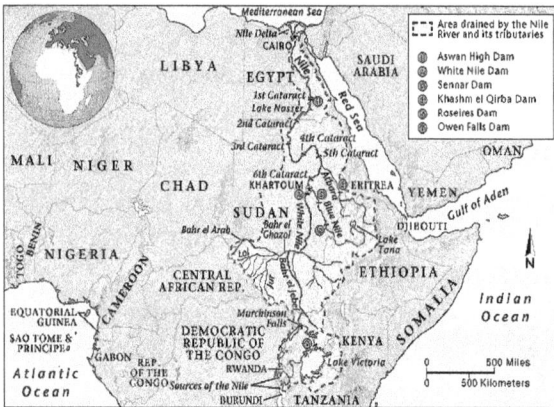

Nile river route in map

Q-101. Which is the largest peninsula in the world?

Ans. Arabia

Q-102. Which is the smallest continent in the world?

Ans. Australia

Q-103. Which is the largest continent in the world?

Ans. Asia

Q-104. Okinawa volcano is situated in which country?

Ans. Japan

Q-105. Where is the 'Death Valley' located?

Ans. California, USA

Death Valley

Q-106. Antigua and Barbuda lie in which Sea?

Ans. Carribean

Q-107. Argentina's east coast lies on which ocean?

Ans. Atlantic Ocean

Q-108. Which South American Canal joins the Atlantic to the Pacific oceans?

Ans. Panama

Q-109. Madagascar is of which coast of Africa?

Ans. East coast

Q-110. What is the Great Barrier Reef made from?

Ans. Corals

Q-111. The Victoria Falls are shared between Zimbabwe and which other country beginning with the same letter Z?

Ans. Zamibia

Q-112. The Channel Tunnel links England with which European country?

Ans. France

Q-113. Which Chinese landmark was viewed from space?

Ans. The Great Wall of China

The Great Wall of China

Q-114. Ottawa is which country's capital?

Ans. Canada

Q-115. Edinburgh is situated in which country?

Ans. Scotland

Q-116. Which is the Largest Zoo in the World?

Ans. Kruger National Park, South Africa

Q-117. What desert does Botswana, Namibia and South Africa have in common?

Ans. The Kalahari

Q-118. Where is Gobi desert situated?

Ans. Mongolia/ Northeastern China

TRIVIA

Choi Jong-yul, a south Korean, is believed to say that he walked across 4,588-mile dune-laden expanse of Sahara Desert "because it was there."

Q-119. Which is the highest waterfall in the World?

Ans. Angel Falls, Venezuela

Q-120. Which is the biggest island of the world?

Ans. Greenland

Q-121. Madagascar is popularly known as the island of what?

Ans. Cloves

Q-122. Which island boasts of Mount Fuji?

Ans. Honshu

Mount Fuji

Q-123. What's the world's highest island mountain?

Ans. Maun Kea

Q-124. Christmas Island is surrounded by which ocean?

Ans. Indian Ocean

Q-125. What Pacific atoll got its name from its location between America and Asia?

Ans. The Midway Islands

Q-126. What makes international boundary between Tanzania and Uganda?

Ans. Victoria Lake

Q-127. Which is the largest Saltwater Lake?

Ans. Caspian Sea

Q-128. Which is the Highest Lake?

Ans. Titicaca

Q-129. Which is the highest mountain in the world?

Ans. Everest

Q-130. After whom is Mount Everest named?

Ans. Sir George Everest

Sir George Everest

Q-131. Which mountain is known as the 'Tiger of the Alps'?

Ans. The Matterhorn

Q-132. Which is the lowest mountain range in the world?

Ans. Buena Bhaile.

Q-133. Which river carries maximum quantity of water into the sea?

Ans. River Amazon

TRIVIA

River Nile is the longest river in the world. It covers approximately 6,695 km and flows through Uganda, Ethiopia, Sudan, Burundi and Egypt. It has two tributaries. Its source is in Sudan, Central Africa and it flows out into the Mediterranean Sea, through Egypt.

Q-134. The river Jordan flows out into which sea?

Ans. Dead Sea

Q-135. Which is the biggest delta in the world?

Ans. Sundarban – the delta of Ganga and Brahmaputra

Sundarban Delta

Q-136. Through which country river Wangchu flows?

Ans. Myanmar

Q-137. What is the length of the English Channel?

Ans. 564 kilometres

Q-138. Where does river Volga flow into?

Ans. Caspian Sea

Q-139. Which capital city stands on the river Danube?

Ans. Belgrade

Q-140. Which stretch of water separates Alaska from Russia?

Ans. The Bering Strait

Q-141. Which river flows through Baghdad?

Ans. River Tigris

Q-142. What kind of a valley Narmada flows through in India?

Ans. V-shaped Fluvial Valley

Q-143. Which is the longest river in North America?

Ans. River Mississippi Missouri

Q-144. On the bank of which river is Montreal situated?

Ans. River Ottawa

Q-145. What do Americans call the Huang Ho, China's second-longest river?

Ans. The Yellow river

Q-146. The Clifton Suspension bridge spans which river?

Ans. The Avon

Clifton Suspension bridge

Q-147. What is the name of the stretch of water between the English mainland and the Isle of Wight?

Ans. The Solent

Q-148. Which is the lowest point on earth?

Ans. The coastal area of Dead Sea

Q-149. The Crimean Peninsular juts into which sea?

Ans. The Black Sea

Q-150. Which canal connects Baltic Sea and North Sea?

Ans. Kiel Canal

Q-151. In which sea Sunda Trench lies?

Ans. The Indian Ocean

Q-152. Which is the largest Ocean?

Ans. Pacific Ocean

Q-153. Which country has the longest coastline in the world?

Ans. Canada

Q-154. Which is the largest bay in the world?

Ans. Hudson Bay, Canada

Hudson Bay

Q-155. Which is the smallest ocean in the world?

Ans. Arctic Ocean

TRIVIA

The Arctic Ocean is the smallest ocean in the world with a total surface area of 5,105,700 sq. miles.

Q-156. Java Island is located in which ocean?

Ans. Indian Ocean

Q-157. Where is Bermuda Triangle located?

Ans. It's located between Bermuda, Florida and Puerto Rico

TRIVIA

The triangular sea area between Bermuda, Florida and Puerto Rico is called the Bermuda Triangle where the currents are very strong. The area gained notoriety in the 1960s on account of the mysterious disappearance of numerous ships and aircraft without any trace of wreckage.

Q-158. Dublin is situated at the mouth of which river?

Ans. River Liffey

Q-159. Which is the largest river in France?

Ans. River Loire

SPORTS

Q-1. Who was the first Test Centurion in Indian cricket?

Ans. Lala Amarnath

Lala Amarnath

Q-2. Who is the first Indian cricketer to score an international triple century in test match?

Ans. Virender Sehwag

Q-3. Which city hosted the first Afro-Asian games?

Ans. Hyderabad

Q-4. Who is the first Indian to take hat-trick in international test cricket?

Ans. Harbhajan Singh

Q-5. With which sports is Jayanta Talukdar associated?

Ans. Archery

Q-6. Who carried Indian Tricolour at Guangzhou Asian Games?

Ans. Gagan Narang

Q-7. Duleep trophy is associated with which sport?

Ans. Cricket

Q-8. Which Indian wrestler won a silver medal in London Olympics 2012?

Ans. Sushil Kumar

Q-9. Who is the first Indian woman athlete to reach the final of an Olympic event?

Ans. P. T. Usha

Q-10. Who was the first athlete to be awarded 'Padma Shree'?

Ans. Bandhu Singh

Q-11. Who got the First Arjuna Award in the field of Athletics?

Ans. G. S. Randhawa

Q-12. Who was the first Indian woman to take part in Olympic Games?

Ans. Merry La RO

Q-13. Name the Indian who won the Olympic silver medal for the first time in shooting event?

Ans. Major Rajyavardhan Rathore

Major Rajyavardhan Rathore

Q-14. Name the Indian who won the Olympic gold medal for the first time in shooting event?

Ans. Abhinav Bindra

Q-15. Where and in which year were the first Asian games held?

Ans. 1951, New Delhi, India

Q-16. Who is the first Indian woman athlete to win gold medal in Asian games?

Ans. Kamal Jeet Sandhu, 1970

Q-17. In which Commonwealth Games did India take part for the first time?

Ans. London, 1934

Q-18. Who won five gold medals in eighteenth Commonwealth Games in shooting event?

Ans. Samresh Jang

Q-19. Name the Indian table tennis player who won gold medal in 18th Commonwealth Games.

Ans. Achanta Sharat Kamal

Achanta Sharat Kamal

Q-20. In which Commonwealth Games did flying Sikh Milkha Singh win the first gold medal for India?

Ans. 1958, Cardiff

Q-21. Lender Paes clinched his career's 50th title at Miami Opens. Whom did he win the doubles title with?

Ans. Radek Stepanek

Q-22. Geeta Poghat, qualified for London Olympics 2012 belongs to which sports?

Ans. Wrestling

Geeta Poghat

Q-23. 'The Colonel' is the name of which Indian test cricketer?

Ans. Dilip Vengsarkar

Q-24. Deodhar Trophy is related to which sport?

Ans. Cricket

Q-25. The Test cricket match in which Rahul Dravid completed his 34th Century was played against which country?

Ans. England

Q-26. Who is the winner of Asia Cup Cricket 2012?

Ans. Pakistan

Q-27. Vijender Singh is associated with which sport?

Ans. Boxing

Q-28. Saina Nehwal plays which sport?

Ans. Badminton

Q-29. How many players does a kabbadi team have?

Ans. Seven players

Q-30. Sachin Tendulkar scored his 50th Test Century in which country?

Ans. South Africa

Q-31. Who is the first Indian woman to win gold at the World Shooting Championship, Munich, Germany?

Ans. Tejaswini Sawant

Q-32. Which award is given for excellence in the field of sports?

Ans. Dhyanchand Award

Q-33. Who is the first Indian to win PGA title of golf?

Ans. Arjun Atwal

Arjun Atwal

Q-34. Who made the fastest hundred in Cricket World Cup 2011?

Ans. K. J. O'Brein

Q-35. Which is the top sports award in India?

Ans. Rajiv Gandhi Khel Ratna

Q-36. Sayali Gokhale is associated with which game/sport?

Ans. Badminton

Q-37. The 'Dronacharya Award' is given to whom?

Ans. Coaches

Q-38. In which Indian state did the game of Polo originate?

Ans. Manipur

Q-39. Khong Kangjei is a Manipuri version of which sport?

Ans. Hockey

Q-40. How many gold medals did P.T. Usha win in the 1986 Seoul Asian Games?

Ans. Four

P. T. Usha

Q-41. India reached the final of the Davis Cup for the first time in which year?

Ans. 1966

Q-42. The name Kunjarani Devi is associated with which sport?

Ans. Weight Lifting

Q-43. Who was the first Indian to reach the semi final in Wimbledon Tennis Championship?

Ans. Ramnathan Krishnan

Q-44. Who was the first Indian to win the World Amateur Billiards title?

Ans. Wilson Jones

Wilson Jones

Q-45. India won its first Olympic hockey gold in which year?

Ans. 1928

Q-46. The Indian football team made its first appearance at Olympics in which year?

Ans. 1948

Q-47. Where did India play its 1st one day international match?

Ans. Headingley

TRIVIA

India lost the match by four wickets on 13-07-1974. Brijesh Patel (82) was the top scorer.

Q-48. Who was the 1st president of BCCI (Board of Control for Cricket in India)?

Ans. R. E. Grant Govan

Q-49. Who was the first Indian world champion in any sport discipline?

Ans. Wilson Jones

Q-50. Who is the first Indian to win the All England Badminton Championship?

Ans. Prakash Padukone, 1980

Q-51. In which Olympics Milkha Singh finished in the 400m final?

Ans. Rome Olympics, 1960

Q-52. In which Olympics did Indian Hockey team win its first gold medal?

Ans. Amsterdam Olympics, 1928

Q-53. Who was independent India's first Olympic medal winner?

Ans. Kashabha DadaSaheb Jadhav

Q-54. Which is the first Asian team to enter semi-finals of football in Olympics?

Ans. India at Melbourne Olympics, 1956

Q-55. Who is the first Asian to swim the English Channel?

Ans. Mihir Sen

Q-56. Who is the first Indian woman to win a medal at the world athletic championship?

Ans. Anju Bobby George (long jump)

Q-57. Who scored highest number of individual goals in hockey in the Olympic championship?

Ans. Roop Singh

TRIVIA

Roop Singh scored 10 goals for India against USA at Los Angeles Olympics in 1932

Q-58. Tennis star Leander Paes won bronze medal in which Olympics?

Ans. Atlanta Olympics, 1996

Q-59. Who won two silver medals for British India in Paris Olympics in 1900?

Ans. Norman Pritchad

Q-60. Who was the first Asian to receive the Helms trophy for the best performance in amateur sports?

Ans. Kunwar Digvijay Singh Babu

Q-61. Who won bronze medal in Sydney Olympics in the 69 kg women's weightlifting?

Ans. Karnam Malleshwari

Karnam Malleshwari

Q-62. Who is the first Indian Grandmaster in chess?

Ans. Vishwanathan Anand

Q-63. Who is the first person to ski down the Mount Everest?

Ans. Yuichiro Miura of Japan

Q-64. Which Indian player scored three successive centuries in three successive test matches?

Ans. Mohammad Azharuddin

Q-65. Who is the first Indian woman to win gold medal in world cup of Archery?

Ans. Dola Bannerji

Q-66. Which Indian female sportsperson registered a win in the Wimbledon?

Ans. Sania Mirza in 2003

Q-67. Name the player of India's Under-19 team under whose captaincy India won the U-19 world cup final 2012.

Ans. Unmukt Chand

Q-68. Name the winning team of the 23rd Federation Cup National Throwball Championship.

Ans. Delhi

Q-69. How many medals did India win in London Olympics 2012.

Ans. Six

Q-70. In London Olympics, Sushil Kumar won a silver medal in Men's wrestling event. In which wrestling event he won the medal?

Ans. 66 Kg Freestyle

Q-71. Who was appointed as the head of Rajiv Gandhi Khel Ratna Awards Committee?

Ans. Rajyavardhan Singh Rathore

Q-72. London Olympic medalists, shooter _____ and Wrestler Yogeshwar Dutt have been awarded the country's highest sporting honour "Rajiv Gandhi Kel Ratna".

Ans. Vijay Kumar

Q-73. Who was the Indian flag bearer in London Olympics 2012?

Ans. Sushil Kumar

Q-74. How many athletes were parts of Indian contingent for London Olympics 2012?

Ans. 81 (Eighty One)

Q-75. Who was announced as the youngest Chess Grandmaster in India on 1 July 2006?

Ans. Parimarjan Negi

Q-76. Which Indian player won Thailand Open Grand Prix Gold title in Bangkok 2012?

Ans. Saina Nehwal

Q-77. Who won the Asian junior wrestling championship in 2012?

Ans. Indu Chaughury and Sakshi Malik

Q-78. Indu Chaudhary and Sakshi Malik won gold Medals in Asian Junior Wrestling Championship 2012. Asian Junior Wrestling Championship 2012 was organised in which country?

Ans. Kazakhastan

Q-79. Which Indian cricketer was conferred upon the Wisdon India Outstanding Achievement award in Dubai on 11 June 2012?

Ans. Sachin Tendulkar

Q-80. Who inaugurated the newly established Sports Science Centre at the LNCPE on 24 May 2012?

Ans. Ajay Maken

Q-81. Kolkata Knight Riders claimed its first ever IPL title on 27 May 2012. The final match of the IPL Five was played in which city?

Ans. Chennai

Q-82. Which Football Club announced to open its first official football school in India?

Ans. Barcelona

Q-83. India won the bronze medal at the junior Asia Cup hockey tournament; the Indian side defeated which nation to claim the bronze?

Ans. South Korea

Q-84. FIFA is an organisation working in which sports field?

Ans. Football

Q-85. What is the full form of FIFA?

Ans. Federation International Football Association

Q-86. After a gap of how many years are Olympics games organized?

Ans. Every four years

Olympic Logo

Q-87. How many squares are there in a chess board?

Ans. Sixty four

Q-88. The term 'Grand Slam' is associated with which sports?

Ans. Lawn Tennis

Q-89. The term '16 yards hit' is associated with which sports?

Ans. Hockey

Q-90. With which game is the 'Double Fault' associated?

Ans. Lawn Tennis

Q-91. In cricket, what is the length of the pitch between the two wickets?

Ans. 22 yards

Q-92. Who broke Pete Sampras's record of maximum Grand Slams in tennis?

Ans. Roger Federer

Roger Federer

Q-93. Meredeka Cup is associated with which sports?

Ans. Football

Q-94. Which game is Ian Thorpe associated with?

Ans. Swimming

Q-95. Where was the first one-day Cricket World Cup held?

Ans. England

Q-96. Topolino Trophy is associated with which sports?

Ans. Golf

Q-97. Asafa Powell, the 100-m race world record holder, is from which country?

Ans. Jamaica

Asafa Powell

Q-98. Scissor kick is associated with which sport?

Ans. Football

Q-99. Tiger Woods is associated with which sport?

Ans. Golf

Q-100. What is the full form of ICC?

Ans. International Council of Cricket

Q-101. What is the other name for Athletics?

Ans. Track and fields

Q-102. What is the direction of running in athletics?

Ans. From left hand side

Athletic track

Q-103. When and where the first Commonwealth Games were held?

Ans. 1930, Hamilton

Q-104. When did the ancient Olympic game start?

Ans. 776 B.C.

Q-105. How many Olympic Games have been organized till now?

Ans. 29

Q-106. When did the first modern Olympic games start?

Ans. 1896

Q-107. Who was the father of Modern Olympic Games?

Ans. Baron pierre De Coubertin

Baron pierre De Coubertin

Q-108. Where the Asian games have been held four times?

Ans. Bangkok

Q-109. How many hurdles are placed in a Hurdle race in one lap?

Ans. Ten

Q-110. How many athletes may be used as substitutes in Relays race event?

Ans. One athlete

Q-111. The procedure of doping test is including the collection of what?

Ans. Urine sample

Q-112. Zinedine Zidane is associated with which sports?

Ans. Football

Q-113. Where will the 2018 FIFA World cup be held?

Ans. Russia

Q-114. Which country won the World Ice Hockey Championship 2012?

Ans. Russia

Q-115. Which sportsperson has won the record Gold medals of Olympic Games?

Ans. Michael Phelps

Michael Phelps

Q-116. Chelsea is a _____ club.

Ans. Football

Q-117. Who was the first heavy weight boxer to go undefeated throughout his career?

Ans. Rocky Marciano

Q-118. Where is the Headquarters of the International Olympic Committee?

Ans. Switzerland

Q-119. Who clinched the FIDE World Cup of Chess in September 2011?

Ans. Peter Svilder

Q-120. Which country led the medals tally in IAAF World Athletics Championship held in Daegu recently?

Ans. USA

Q-121. Who is the winner of Tour Championship and Fed Ex Cup of golf?

Ans. Bill Haas

Q-122. Samantha Stosur won her first UP Open (Women's Singles) Tennis Championship. Where does she belong to?

Ans. Australia

Samantha Stosur

Q-123. Novak Djokovic won the Wimbledon 2011 Men's Singles title after defeating whom?

Ans. Rafael Nadal

Q-124. Who is the top run getter in Cricket World Cup 2011?

Ans. TM Dilshan

Q-125. Who won the Australian Open Women's Singles title 2011?

Ans. Kim Klijsters

Q-126. Where is the Wanderers Test Cricket ground located?

Ans. Johannesburg

Q-127. Athletes with higher proportion of red fibres in their muscles are better equipped for which sport?

Ans. Swimming

Q-128. Bull Fighting is the national game of which country?

Ans. Spain

Bull fighting

Q-129. The term 'Bishop' is related to which game?

Ans. Chess

Q-130. Which country clinched the Women Hockey World Cup in 2010?

Ans. Argentina

Q-131. Maradona is a Famous Football Player of which Country?

Ans. Argentina

Q-132. Which country led a boycott of the 1980 Olympic Games held in Moscow?

Ans. USA

Q-133. The first World Cup in cricket was held in which year?

Ans. 1975

Q-134. Which cricketer holds the record of highest individual score in One-Day Internationals (ODIs)?

Ans. Sachin Tendulkar

Q-135. What is the distance of running in a marathon race?

Ans. 26 miles 385 yards

Q-136. Which Major League Baseball player holds the record for all-time career high batting average?

Ans. Ty Cobb

Q-137. Which NBA player scored 8 points in the final 7 seconds of a game to lead his team to victory?

Ans. Reggie Miller

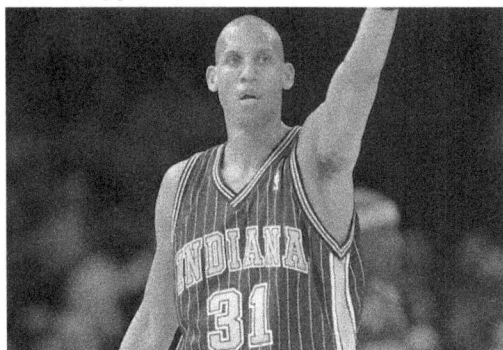

Reggie Miller

Q-138. Who beat Duke in the Great Alaskan Shootout Finals in 1998?

Ans. University of Cincinnati

Q-139. The first hang gliders were flown in which century?

Ans. 19th century

Q-140. Which track and field star overcame childhood polio to become one of the greatest athletes of her time?

Ans. Wilma Rudolph

Q-141. Who was the youngest world heavy-weight boxing champion?

Ans. Mike Tyson

Q-142. In golf, what is meant by the term 'birdie'?

Ans. One under par

Q-143. How many red balls are used in a game of snooker?

Ans. 15

Q-144. Name the player who scored the final goal of the 1966 Football World Cup Final?

Ans. Geoff Hurst

Geoff Hurst in 1966

Q-145. In motor racing, which flag is waved to show the winner?

Ans. Black and white chequered flag

Q-146. In Lawn tennis, what is the point score immediately after deuce?

Ans. Advantage

Q-147. What is the official name of the Rugby World Cup trophy?

Ans. The William Webb Ellis Trophy

Q-148. What is Zumba?

Ans. Latin American dance based workout

Q-149. What was the name of the England footballer to become the first European Footballer of the Year?

Ans. Stanley Matthews

Stanley Matthews

Q-150. In darts, how high off the floor must the bull's eye measures?

Ans. 5 feet, 8 inches

Q-151. Which country invented volleyball?

Ans. USA

Q-152. Which colour is an archery target centre?

Ans. Gold

Q-153. What is the highest possible score with three darts?

Ans. 180

Q-154. What height is the centre of Lawn tennis net in feet?

Ans. Three feet

Q-155. In a rugby league team, how many players are there?

Ans. 13

Rugby team

Q-156. Which sport is associated with Constantino Rocca?

Ans. Golf

Q-157. Where was the FIFA World Cup held in 1986?

Ans. Mexico

Q-158. Which horse won the Melbourne Cup in 2002?

Ans. Media Puzzle

Q-159. Which country did Baseball originate from?

Ans. England

Q-160. How many pockets does a snooker table have?

Ans. 6

Q-161. Who won the 2003 British Open golf tournament?

Ans. Ben Curtis

Q-162. What is the height and width of a football goalpost?

Ans. Height = 2.4m / Width = 7.3m

Q-163. How many holes are there in a standard ten pin bowling ball?

Ans. Three

Q-164. Which country hosted the Football World Cup in 2006?

Ans. Germany

CINEMA

Q-1. Which was the first Indian Talkie film?

Ans. Alam Ara

Poster of Alam Ara

Q-2. The first Indian Talkie film, Alam Ara, is directed by whom?

Ans. Ardeshi Irani

Q-3. Which is the first 70 mm film of India?

Ans. Around the World, released in 1967.

Q-4. Which is the first Cinemascope film of India?

Ans. Kaaghaz Ke Phool (1959)

Q-5. Which is the first Panavision film of India?

Ans. Shalimar (1978)

Q-6. Who won the first 'Dada Sahab Phalke' award?

Ans. Devika Rani

Q-7. Which is the first film to be made in Sanskrit language?

Ans. Adi Sankara, directed by G.V. Ayyar in 1983

Q-8. Which is the first silent feature film of India?

Ans. Raja Harishchandra

Q-9. Who is known as the 'Father of Indian Cinema'?

Ans. Dhundiraj Govind Phalke, better known as Dada Sahab Phalke.

Dada Sahab Phalke

Q-10. Who is the first Indian to win Oscar award?

Ans. Bhanu Athaiya for Best dress designing for Richard Attenborough's film 'Gandhi'

Bhanu Athaiya

Q-11. In which year was National Award constituted?

Ans. In the year 1954

Q-12. Which is the first complete Technicolour film of India?

Ans. Jhansi Ki Rani (1953)

Q-13. Which is the first Cinema Theatre of India?

Ans. Elphinstone Palace (1907) in Calcutta (now Kolkata)

Q-14. Which is the first English film of Indian Cinema?

Ans. The Court Dancer

Q-15. Which is the first indigenously made film of India?

Ans. Sholay (1975) by G.P. Sippy

Q-16. Who directed 'Raja Harishchandra'?

Ans. Dada Saheb Phalke

Poster of Raja Harishchandra

Q-17. Which is the biggest film studio in India?

Ans. Ramoji film studio, Hyderabad.

Q-18. Which is the first Indian film without songs?

Ans. Naujawan (1937) by JBH Wadia

Q-19. Who was the music director of Pather Panchali?

Ans. Pandit Ravi Shankar

Q-20. Which Indian film has the maximum number of songs?

Ans. Indra Sabha

TRIVIA

Indra Sabha has record number of 71 songs.

Q-21. Which is the first Indian film to win an international award?

Ans. Pather Panchali by Satyajit Ray

Satyajit Ray

Q-22. Pather Panchali was based on a novel by which author?

Ans. It was based on Bibhutibhushan Bandhopadhyay's novel by the same name.

Q-23. Which is the first 3D film of India?

Ans. 'My Dear Kuttichatthan' (1984). It is a Malayalam film directed by Navodaya appachan.

Q-24. When and where was the first Film Festival of India held?

Ans. In 1954, Bombay (now Mumbai)

Q-25. Which Indian sound Engineer won an Oscar award?

Ans. Resul Pookkutty for Slumdog Millionaire in 2009

Q-26. Which music director won Oscar for India?

Ans. A. R. Rehman for Slumdog Millionaire, 2009

A. R. Rehman

TRIVIA

A. R Rehman won two awards – Best Original Song and Best Original Music score – in 2009 for the film Slumdog Millionaire, in the 81st Academy awards, popularly known as Oscar awards.

Q-27. Who was the first actor to become the chief Minister of a state?

Ans. M. G. Ramchandran, popularly known as M.G.R

Q-28. Who was the first actress to become the Chief Minister of a state?

Ans. Janaki Ramachandran.

TRIVIA

Janaki Ramchandran was the wife of MG Ramachandran who later succeeded him as the Chief Minister of Tamil Nadu, after his death. However, her government lasted only 24 days.

Q-29. Name the only Bengali film produced by the late Raj Kapoor.

Ans. Ek Din Raatre

Q-30. Where is the Film & Television Institute of India (FTII) situated?

Ans. Pune

FTII

Q-31. Which renowned film actress was the subject of the painting 'Nautanki'?

Ans. Madhuri Dixit

Q-32. Begum Ayesha Sultana is popularly known in the Indian film world as _____.

Ans. Sharmila Tagore

Q-33. Which Indian dancer-actress played the role of Draupadi in Peter Brook's internationally acclaimed version of the Mahabharata?

Ans. Mallika Sarabhai

Mallika Sarabhai

Q-34. Which legendary playback singer made his debut in Hindi films with the film 'Anandmath' made in 1951?

Ans. Hemant Kumar

Q-35. Ajaya Singh Deol is the real name of _____.

Ans. Sunny Deol

Q-36. Who was the first Indian female child star?

Ans. Mandakini

Q-37. Who played the first ever double role in Indian cinema?

Ans. Master Vithal

Q-38. Name the only film actress to have received a fan-letter from Jawaharlal Nehru.

Ans. Devika Rani

Q-39. Who was the first music composer to receive the Sangeet Natak Akademi Award?

Ans. S. D. Burman

SD Burman

Q-40. The film 'Kal Aaj Aur Kal' was directed by _____.

Ans. Randhir Kapoor

Q-41. Which Mrinal Sen's film has a shot of Satyajit Ray behind a camera?

Ans. Bhuvan Shome

Q-42. Which noted playwright wrote the screen play for the much acclaimed film 'Manthan'?

Ans. Vijay Tendulkar

Vijay Tendulkar

Q-43. For which film did Shabana Azmi render her voice to sing a song?

Ans. Anjuman

Q-44. The film 'Son of India' was made in 1962 by _____.

Ans. Mehboob Khan

Q-45. Which actor was originally chosen to play the role of 'Gabbar Singh' in the super hit Hindi film 'Sholay' before the role was offered to Amjad Khan?

Ans. Danny Denzongpa

Q-46. Who performed Bharat Natyam during the very first Film Fare Awards ceremony in 1954?

Ans. Vyjyanthimala

Q-47. For which film did Amitabh Bachchan win his first Filmfare Best Actor trophy?

Ans. Amar Akbar Anthony

Q-48. Which famous director scored two hat-tricks winning the Filmfare Best Director trophy for the years 1953, 1954, 1955 and 1958, 1959 and 1960?

Ans. Bimal Roy

Bimal Roy

Q-49. Who was the first actor to receive the Filmfare Best Actor award and the Critics' Award for Best Actor in the same year?

Ans. Shahrukh Khan

Q-50. Which Indian film bagged five awards at the 13th Valenciennes International Film Festival in France?

Ans. Kabhi Khushi Kabhi Gham

Q-51. Which film company was launched by Dada Saheb Phalke?

Ans. Hindustan Cinema Films Co.

Dada Saheb Phalke

Q-52. The first full-length motion picture in India was produced by _____.

Ans. Dada Saheb Phalke

Q-53. The first Indian Talking Film was released in the year _____.

Ans. 1931

Q-54. Which period is considered as the "Golden Age of Indian cinema", during which time some of the most critically acclaimed Indian films of all time were produced?

Ans. 1940s to 1960s

Q-55. The 'Apu Trilogy' was a trilogy consisting of three Bengali films, which established Indian parallel cinema, was directed by whom?

Ans. Satyajit Ray

Poster of Pather Panchali

Q-56. Satyajit Ray, regarded as one of the greatest auteurs of the 20th century cinema, won how many National Film Awards?

Ans. 32 National Film Awards

Q-57. The Indian Masala film, slang used for commercial films with song, dance, romance, etc., came up following what major event?

Ans. Second World War

Q-58. South Indian cinema gained prominence throughout India with the release of _____.

Ans. S.S. Vasan's Chandralekha

Q-59. The lead female role in the popular Hindi Movie "Mother India" which was released in 1957 was portrayed by _____.

Ans. Nargis

Q-60. In which year was the Filmfare award inaugurated?

Ans. In the year 1951

Filmfare trophy

Q-61. Which actress won the debut Filmfare award for her debut film as the main lead?

Ans. Meena Kumari won for her debut performance as main lead in Baiju Bawra.

Q-62. Who was the first female director of Hindi films?

Ans. Begum Fatima Sultana

Q-63. Which was the first Punjabi talkie film?

Ans. Heer Ranjha in year 1932

Q-64. Which was the first Marathi film?

Ans. Ayodhyacha Raja by V. Shantaram

Q-65. Which was the first film production house in hindi films?

Ans. Bombay Talkies headed by Himanshu Rai and Devika Rani

TRIVIA

Central Board of Film Censors was formed in 1951 with B.N. Sircar on the Board.

Q-66. Who enacted the role of child Raj Kapoor in the film Awara?

Ans. Shashi Kapoor

Q-67. Which famous film personality was born as Balraj Dutt?

Ans. Sunil Dutt

Q-68. Which popular film star acted in the TV series 'Circus'?

Ans. Shahrukh Khan

Q-69. What is common between 'Pyaasa', 'Kaaghaz Ke Phool' and 'Baazi'?

Ans. They all had actor-director Guru Dutt as their main lead.

Guru Dutt

Q-70. Which was considered as India's largest and most influential film company in the silent era?

Ans. Kohinoor film company

Q-71. Which famous female actor of the yester-years was the daughter of the Parsi theatre actor Ali Bux and dancer Iqbal Begum?

Ans. Meena Kumari

Meena Kumari

Q-72. What is IPTA?

Ans. Indian People's Theatre Association

Q-73. When was IPTA founded?

Ans. In 1942, during the Quit India movement

Q-74. Name the first film produced by IPTA.

Ans. Dharti Ke Lal in 1949

Q-75. Which was the first monochrome film to be fully converted into colour in 2004?

Ans. Mughal-E-Azam

Q-76. Which Indian movie made its entry into Oscar Awards in 2003?

Ans. Devdas

Q-77. Which was the first Hindi Movie to receive the national award?

Ans. Mirza Ghalib

Q-78. Which playback singer has been awarded the Bharat Ratna, the nation's highest civilian honour?

Ans. Lata Mangeshkar

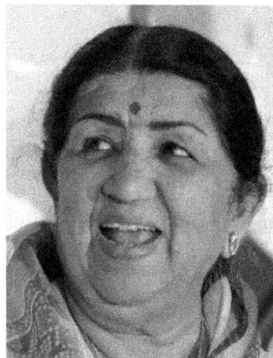

Lata Mangeshkar

Q-79. Which music director brought Indian classical music into the film medium?

Ans. Naushad

Q-80. Bimal Roy's classic 'Do Bigha Zameen' is inspired by which film?

Ans. The Bicycle Thief

Q-81. Who was the director of 'The Bicycle Thief'?

Ans. Vittorio De Sica

Vittorio De Sica

Q-82. Who wrote the iconic "Ae mere pyaare watan…"?

Ans. Prem Dhawan

Q-83. On which story is the film Kabuliwala based?

Ans. Rabindranath Tagore's Kabuliwala

Q-84. Which song sung by Lata Mangeshkar reportedly moved Pandit Jawahar Lal Nehru to tears?

Ans. "Ae mere watan ke logon…"

Q-85. Which film was reportedly based on the Indo-Sino war of 1965?

Ans. Haqeeqat by Vijay Anand

Q-86. On whose novel was the film Sahib Bibi Aur Ghulam based?

Ans. Bimal Mitra's Saheb Bibi Gholam

Poster of Sahib Bibi Aur Ghulam

Q-87. Who directed the epic Mughal-E-Azam?

Ans. K. Asif

TRIVIA

Bombay Film Society was the first film society in India formed in Bombay in 1942.

Q-88. Who won the 2011 Oscar for Best actor?

Ans. Colin Firth for his role in the film 'The King's Speech'

poster of 'The King's Speech'

Q-89. Who won the 2011 Oscar for Best actress?

Ans. Natalie Portman for her role in the film Black Swan

Q-90. Which film won the 2011 Oscar for the best film?

Ans. The King's Speech

Q-91. What is the film title of the sequel to Alice In Wonderland?

Ans. Through The Looking Glass

Q-92. Which famous actress was born as Norma Jeane Mortenson?

Ans. Marilyn Monroe

Marilyn Monroe

Q-93. Who played James Bond in 'Live and Let Die'?

Ans. Roger Moore

Q-94. How many 'Rocky' films did Sylvester Stallone star in?

Ans. 6

Q-95. What are the names of Snow White's seven dwarfs?

Ans. Sneezy, Happy, Grumpy, Sleepy, Bashful, Dopey, Doc

Q-96. What was the name of the boy in the Jungle Book?

Ans. Mowgli

Q-97. In the film 'Shrek', what is the name of Shrek's wife?

Ans. Fiona

Fiona

Q-98. Which James Bond film was named after Ian Fleming's home in Jamaica?

Ans. Goldeneye

Q-99. Which Bond movie did Daniel Craig first star in?

Ans. Casino Royale

Q-100. What is the name of the actor who played the role of Harry Potter in the film series?

Ans. Daniel Radcliffe

Q-101. Who starred as the Tarzan in the first movie?

Ans. Elmo Lincoln

Q-102. Who played Jack in the film 'The Titanic'?

Ans. Leonardo DiCaprio

Q-103. What was the title of the film in which Robin Williams played an English teacher called John Keating?

Ans. Dead Poets Society

Q-104. Who made the quote 'I'll be back' famous?

Ans. Arnold Schwarzenneger

Arnold Schwarzenneger

Q-105. What was the title of the film that starred Elvis Presley playing the role of a boxer?

Ans. Kid Galahad

Q-106. Which Disney film does the song 'Circle of Life' come from?

Ans. The Lion King

Q-107. Which Disney film does the song 'The Bare Necessities' come from?

Ans. The Jungle Book

Q-108. Which film had the quote, "Here's looking at you, kid?"

Ans. Casablanca

Q-109. Which film had lines, "We're bigger than US Steel?"

Ans. The Godfather

The Godfather poster

Q-110. "At my signal, unleash hell," is from which movie?

Ans. Gladiator

Q-111. Which movie did Warren Beatty opt to shoot in seven basic comic book colours?

Ans. Dick Tracy.

Q-112. Which 1995 movie was the first film to feature characters who attend weekly "plastic corrosion awareness meetings"?

Ans. Toy Story.

Q-113. Which 71-year-old actor celebrated his Oscar win by doing a set of One-handed push-ups on stage?

Ans. Jack Palance.

Q-114. Which animated Disney title character, originally modelled after Michael J. Fox, was later retooled to resemble Tom Cruise?

Ans. Aladdin

Q-115. Which was the first animated Disney feature film not based on an existing story?

Ans. The Lion King

Q-116. Which actor got a record 11th Oscar nomination in 1998?

Ans. Jack Nicholson.

Q-117. Which Disney feature film was the first animated film nominated for a Best Picture Oscar?

Ans. Beauty and the Beast.

Q-118. Which updated Disney classic was the first animated feature to appear on giant IMAX screens?

Ans. Fantasia 2000.

Q-119. Harry Potter series is a production of _____

Ans. Warner Brothers

Q-120. What name is associated with the rise of early cinematic shorts?

Ans. Thomas Edison

> ### TRIVIA
> *Edison's company (Edison and Co.) largely headed up the initiative of cinematic shorts, creating well known films such as "The Kiss", "The Strong Man", and "The Execution of Mary, Queen of Scots".*

Q-123. Who was the lead pair in 'Pretty Woman'?

Ans. Richard Gere and Julia Roberts

Q-124. Who was the first actor to play James Bond?

Ans. Sean Connery

Q-125. Who directed 'Gone with the wind'?

Ans. Victor Fleming

Film poster of Gone with the wind

Q-126. Which actor played the role of Spiderman first?

Ans. Tobey Maguire

Q-127. Who directed the first Harry Potter film in the series, Harry Potter and the Philosopher's stone?

Ans. Chris Columbus

Q-128. Richard Harris played the role of Professor Albus Dumbledore in the first two films of Harry Potter series. Who played this role after his death?

Ans. Michael Gambon

Q-129. What is the most significant thing about the cast of the Harry Potter series?

Ans. All its major cast is British. Most of the actors are either English or Irish.

Q-130. Which Harry Potter character does Gary Oldman plays?

Ans. Sirius Black

Q-131. Who directed Slumdog Millionaire?

Ans. Danny Boyle

Q-132. Which yesteryear actress plays the role of Professor Minerva McGonagall?

Ans. Maggie Smith

Maggie Smith

Q-133. Who directed The Bride and Prejudice?

Ans. Gurinder Chaddha

> **TRIVIA**
>
> *The film Bride and Prejudice is based on Jane Austen's Pride and Prejudice.*

Q-134. How many films are there in the Lord of the Rings series?

Ans. Three

Q-135. James Cameron rose to fame through which directorial work?

Ans. Titanic

Q-136. Who is the director of Avatar, released in 2009?

Ans. James Cameron

> **TRIVIA**
>
> *Cameron started working upon Avatar since 1994. The film was released in 2009.*

Q-137. Who directed the classic E.T.?

Ans. Steven Spielberg

Steven Spielberg

Q-138. Chronicles of Narnia has seen how many releases in the series so far?

Ans. Three

Q-139. Akira Kurosawa was a noted Director, Screenwriter, Editor and Producer. What is his nationality?

Ans. Japanese

Q-140. Alfred Hitchcock, the noted film maker, is famous for making what genre of films?

Ans. Suspense thrillers

Q-141. Majid Majidi is a famous _____ film maker.

Ans. Iranian

Q-142. In which year was the first Cannes film festival held?

Ans. In 1932, Venice

Q-143. In which year was the Golden Palm award started?

Ans. 1955

Q-144. Which film gave Ingrid Bergman a cult status?

Ans. Casablanca

Film Poster of Casablanca

Q-145. Which film was awarded the first Oscar award?

Ans. Wings, in 1928

Q-146. Who directed Wuthering Heights, 1939?

Ans. William Wyler

Q-147. Hailed as a classic, which 1958 film directed by Alfred Hitchcock stars James Stewart and Kim Novak in the lead role?

Ans. Vertigo

Vertigo film poster

Q-148. Which Frank Capra film of 1941 stars Gary Cooper and Edward Arnold? It is one of the 50 classic films of all times.

Ans. Meet John Doe

Q-149. Prior to James Cameron, which other director made Titanic in the year 1953?

Ans. Jean Negulesco

Q-150. Who directed the 1965 classic 'The Sound of Music'?

Ans. Robert Wise

Q-151. Who was the music director of The Sound of Music?

Ans. Richard Rodgers

Q-152. When was the 20th Century Fox founded?

Ans. On May 31, 1935

Q-153. Which male actor won the most Oscars in his career?

Ans. Clint Eastwood

Clint Eastwood

Q-154. Which female actor won the most Oscars in her career?

Ans. Katharine Hepburn

CHILDREN'S ENCYCLOPEDIA
THE WORLD OF KNOWLEDGE

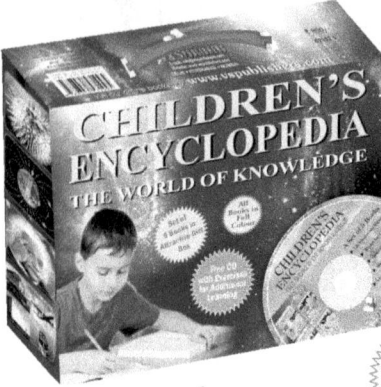

All Books in Full Colour

Free CD for additional reference

Set of 5 Books in Attractive Gift Box

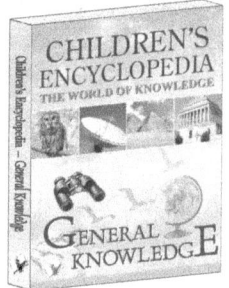

Code: 02152 S

CHILDREN'S ENCYCLOPEDIA — THE WORLD OF KNOWLEDGE — LIFE SCIENCES AND HUMAN BODY

CHILDREN'S ENCYCLOPEDIA — THE WORLD OF KNOWLEDGE — PHYSICS AND CHEMISTRY

CHILDREN'S ENCYCLOPEDIA — THE WORLD OF KNOWLEDGE — SPACE SCIENCE AND ELECTRONICS

CHILDREN'S ENCYCLOPEDIA — THE WORLD OF KNOWLEDGE — SCIENTISTS INVENTIONS AND DISCOVERIES

CHILDREN'S ENCYCLOPEDIA — THE WORLD OF KNOWLEDGE — GENERAL KNOWLEDGE

71 SERIES (71 श्रृंखला)

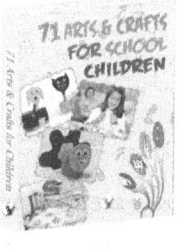

71 + 10 New Mathematics Projects

Spice in Science — The best of Science funnies

71 Electrical & Electronic Projects

71 Famous Scientists — Coming Soon

Greatest Scientists of the World — Coming Soon

World Famous Scientists

71 साइंस प्रोजेक्ट्स

71 + 10 New Science Projects — Self-learning Kit

71 आறிவியல் திட்டங்கள் — Self-learning Kit

71 साइंस एक्सपेरिमेंट्स — 71 Science Experiments

71 Science Experiments

71 + 10 New Science Projects Junior

71 साइंस प्रोजेक्ट्स

71 Science Activities

71 साइंस प्रतिक्रिया

71 + 10 Magic Tricks for Children

71 Arts & Crafts for School Children